BRINGING DINOSAUR BONES TO LIFE

How Do We Know What Dinosaurs Were Like?

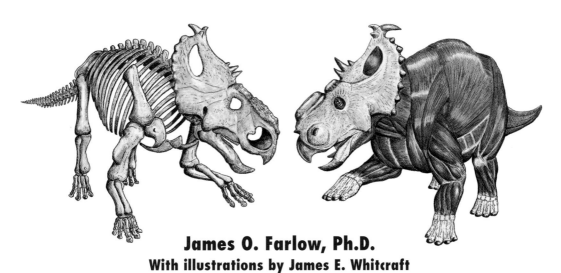

James O. Farlow, Ph.D.
With illustrations by James E. Whitcraft

Franklin Watts
A Division of Scholastic Inc.
New York/Toronto/London/Auckland/Sydney
Mexico City/New Delhi/Hong Kong
Danbury, Connecticut

For John H. Ostrom,
with gratitude for all his help over the years—*J.O.F.*

Photographs ©:American Museum of Natural History: 24 (338951/J. Beckett/Courtesy Dept. of Library Services), 36 (5789/D. Finnin); Bruce Evans: 64; Jaap Hillenius: 13 top; James O. Farlow: 7, 14 top, 21, 26, 34, 37, 39, 44 inset; Jeff Lang: 28; Rick Hudson: 32; Rick Jones: 13 bottom; Smithsonian Institution, Washington, DC: 9 (MNH-26449), 20, 44 (27354); Terry Jones: 12, 14 bottom; U.S. Geological Survey, Denver, CO: 10.

Library of Congress Cataloging-in-Publication Data
Farlow, James Orville.
Bringing dinosaur bones to life : how do we know what dinosaurs were like?/
James O. Farlow; with photographs and illustrations by James E. Whitcraft.
p. cm.
Includes bibliographical references and index.
ISBN 0-531-11403-1
Dinosaurs—Juvenile literature. [1. Dinosaurs.] I. Whitcraft, James E., ill. II. Title.
QE861.5 .F37 2001
567.9-dc21   00-038150

Contents

CHAPTER 1
THINKING ABOUT DINOSAURS

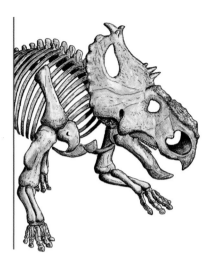

In monster movies, we often see exciting scenes of dinosaurs fighting deadly battles. In dinosaur books, we see illustrations of these great reptiles feeding, sitting on nests, and protecting their young. Sometimes the dinosaurs look dull—in colors of green, gray, or brown. In other pictures, they are colored with all the shades of the rainbow.

A restoration showing a fight between *Alxasaurus* (right) and a large theropod (left).

Well, which pictures are correct? How do we decide what they looked like? *Can* we know what dinosaurs were like as living animals? These questions are what this book is about. Many dinosaur books tell what we know—or think we know—about dinosaurs. This book, however, is about *how* we know it. We will look at how **paleontologists** (scientists who study **fossils** to learn about ancient life) make **interpretations** of what living dinosaurs were like.

To start, scientists make **observations** of their fossils. They look at the shapes and sizes of the bones of a dinosaur skeleton, for example. The bones provide facts about the dinosaur that a paleontologist can use in understanding the animal. From the shape of the dinosaur's teeth, the scientist might guess that it was a plant-eater. From the shapes of its leg bones, she or he might speculate that this kind of dinosaur was a fast runner. From the size of the bones our paleontologist might guess that the dinosaur weighed half a ton.

These speculations are "educated guesses," based on what we know about the effects of bone size and shape on weights, diets, and running abilities in living animals. Scientists try to do more than speculate, however. A speculation becomes a **hypothesis** if the scientist can think of a way to test it. Hypotheses are tested by making new observations, or doing experiments and comparing the results with what the scientist would expect to see if the hypothesis were correct. If new observations are consistent with our hypothesis, we say that they support our hypothesis. For example, the scientist makes a hypothesis that a dinosaur could run quickly. To test the hypothesis, the scientist looks at how strong its leg bones were. Are they strong enough to resist the forces that would act on them if the dinosaur had been a fast runner?

Even if observations support a hypothesis, this does not prove the hypothesis is true. If measurements show that the leg bones of a dinosaur were strong enough for the dinosaur to move quickly, this does not prove the dinosaur was a fast runner. Its leg bones might have been strong for some reason that had nothing to do with running. However, if our measurements show that the dinosaur's leg bones were not strong enough to withstand the stresses of running, the hypothesis that our dinosaur was a fast runner is proven false.

So, we can seldom prove that a hypothesis is true. We can, however, see whether the hypothesis is supported by new observations, or whether new observations disprove it. A good hypothesis is one that can easily be shown to be wrong if it is, in fact, false.

If a hypothesis survives one test, scientists try to think of more tests to either support it or prove it wrong. If the dinosaur has limb bones that were strong enough to support running, we might then look at the joints between the dinosaur's leg bones. Would their shape have allowed the kinds of movements necessary for fast running? Next we might look at the animal's foot, to see if it matches the shape seen in modern animals that are good runners. We could look for fossilized footprints of dinosaurs similar to the one we are studying to see if they are spaced far enough apart to indicate that their maker had been running.

Sometimes, a hypothesis will be consistent with some observations, but not with others. If this happens, scientists have to decide whether the inconsistencies are important enough to prove the hypothesis entirely wrong, or whether the hypothesis only needs slight changes. As

Trackways—fossilized dinosaur footprints—provide scientists with information to support or disprove a hypothesis. This trackway is from a site in Austin, Texas.

you might expect, scientists don't always agree about this! These disagreements often occur when paleontologists try to determine what dinosaurs were like as living animals.

If a hypothesis survives many tests, we have confidence that it is probably true. We call it a **theory**, and consider it a fact that can be used in testing other hypotheses. Even then, however, we are not sure that our theory is correct. Some future test may prove the theory to be incorrect, or only a partial explanation. Until that happens, though—if it ever does—the theory remains our best explanation for the observations that led us to construct the theory.

Some ideas about dinosaurs are easier to test than others. Our present understanding of dinosaurs is a mixture of theories, hypotheses, and untested, educated guesses. We are much more sure about some aspects of dinosaur biology than others. The trick is to know how much confidence we can have in any particular idea about dinosaurs. By the time you have finished this book, you will be ready to think critically about what dinosaurs were like—just as a paleontologist does.

CHAPTER 2
WHAT DID DINOSAURS LOOK LIKE?

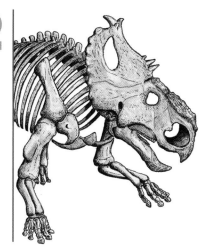

One of the first things we want to know about dinosaurs is what they looked like. How big were they? How were they shaped? What did their skin look like? What color were they? In this chapter, we will look at dinosaur features paleontologists agree about, and we will also look at features about which they disagree.

This drawing of a *Stegosaurus* skeleton shows the bones as they were found. The living animal would be about 20 feet (6 m) long. Well-preserved skeletons like this are necessary in order to make a reconstruction.

When paleontologists think about the appearance of dinosaurs, and try to develop theories about them, they start with two steps. First, they want to make a **reconstruction**—a picture of what a dinosaur's skeleton looks like. To make the reconstruction, a paleontologist needs a fairly complete skeleton of the dinosaur, or at least the skeleton of a closely related dinosaur. A reconstruction based on a good skeleton can help us estimate how long or how tall our dinosaur was.

From the reconstruction, a paleontologist goes on to make a **restoration**—an interpretation of how the dinosaur looked as a living animal. The scientist builds an interpretation of the dinosaur's appearance outward, from the skeleton to the skin. Think of this work as building from the bones (the reconstruction) to the body (the restoration).

Some dinosaur bones show bumps and scars to which—as in living animals—the reptile's muscles were attached by **tendons**. From these clues, and from studies of how muscles are arranged in modern dinosaur relatives (birds and crocodilians), paleontologists make interpretations of the sizes and arrangements of dinosaurs' muscles. These interpretations are a mixture of observations, hypotheses, and educated

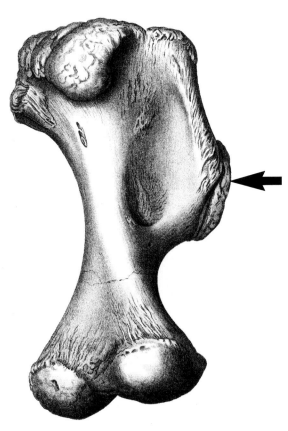

On this drawing of a *Triceratops'* right humerus (upper arm bone), an arrow shows the attachment site of a large arm muscle. The bone is about 30 inches (76 cm) long.

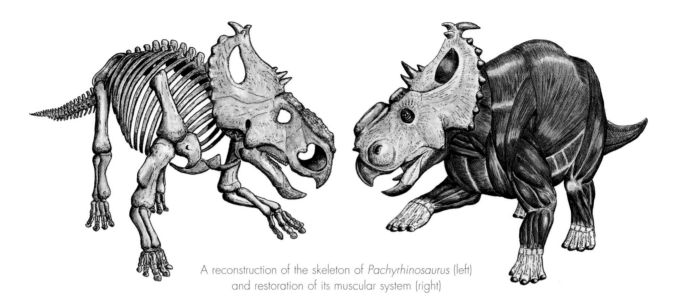

A reconstruction of the skeleton of *Pachyrhinosaurus* (left) and restoration of its muscular system (right)

guesses, and so the restoration of a dinosaur's **musculature** (the arrangement of muscles on its body) is a "well-informed speculation." It may be reasonably accurate as a rough outline, but it is probably wrong in many details.

Similarly, working from what we know about the internal organs of living animals, we make guesses about the size and arrangement of the dinosaur's heart, lungs, stomach, intestines, and other organs. Fortunately, with two little **theropods** (meat-eating dinosaurs)—*Sinosauropteryx* and *Scipionyx*—we can do better than guess about their internal organs. We have discovered skeletons of these dinosaurs that are remarkably well preserved. The rock in which the bones of *Sinosauropteryx* are found show dark regions where the eyes and other organs would have been—probably traces of those very organs! Some scientists think that a dark area in the dinosaur's belly region shows the outline of the

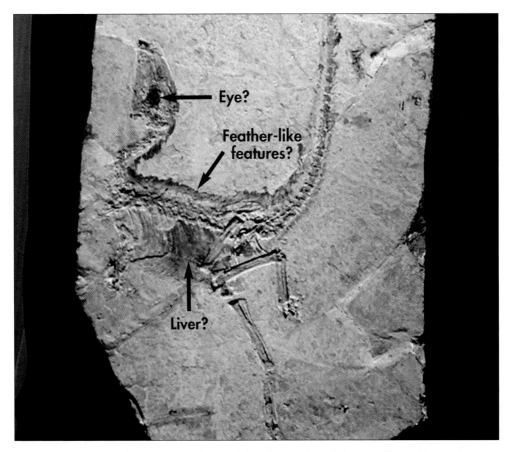

Eye?

Feather-like features?

Liver?

Sinosauropteryx, a small carnivorous dinosaur from China, about 28 inches (70 cm) long. Arrows indicate possible traces of the eye and liver, and small structures that have been interpreted as feather-like features.

dinosaur's liver. If so, the dinosaur's liver was in the same position that it is in living crocodilians. *Scipionyx* shows the same features, and also shows traces of muscles and intestines.

In crocodilians, muscles are attached to the liver, and run from there to bones of the hip. When the muscles contract, they pull the liver back, toward the hip. This in turn pulls the lungs back, causing them to expand and fill with air. Scientists who think that the liver of these theropods was positioned in the same way, also think that these dinosaurs, like crocodilians, used backward and forward movement of the liver to help in breathing. If this interesting hypothesis survives further testing, it will be one of the few cases where fossils show us how a dinosaur's internal organs worked. However, many paleontologists

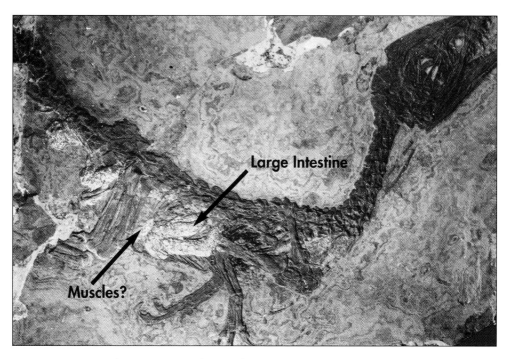

Top: *Scipionyx*, an infant carnivorous dinosaur from Italy; skull length about 2 inches (55 mm). Arrows indicate the large intestine and possible remnants of muscles running from the hipbones to the liver. Bottom: Diagram of an alligator, showing the lung, liver, and muscles running from the liver to the hipbones. Some paleontologists think that theropod dinosaurs had a similar arrangement of soft tissues associated with breathing.

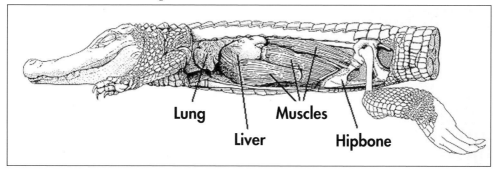

doubt that the liver in *Sinosauropteryx* has been correctly identified. They also question whether it played a part in filling the lungs.

For some kinds of dinosaurs, pieces of the animal's skin left impressions in the sediment that packed around the dinosaur's body after it died. The sediment turned to stone and preserved a trace of the dinosaur's skin. From these impressions we see that some dinosaurs had skin with pebbly scales and bony knobs, much like the skin of living crocodilians. Some dinosaurs also had frills of skin running along the back, as do many modern lizards. Other dinosaurs had knobby ridges of bone along the back.

But when we look at fossils of *Sinosauropteryx*, however, we see that this dinosaur may have had a very different body covering. Its skeletons have a fringe of fiber-like structures running along the top of the dinosaur's head and neck, and along its back, and down the top and bottom of its tail. These structures may have covered other parts of the body, too. Most paleontologists think that these are the remains of the animal's body covering, and that they may even be simple feather-like features. If so, *Sinosauropteryx* and related theropods would have looked very different from what paleontologists earlier thought.

Some scientists, however, believe that the fiber-like structures of *Sinosauropteryx* are really the remains of tissues that were beneath the dinosaur's skin, and were not the animal's actual body covering. If this interpretation is correct, then the skin of *Sinosauropteryx* may not have been so different from that of other dinosaurs.

How can we choose between these two hypotheses? We could examine the fiber-like structures under very high magnification, to see if their size, structure, and arrangement is like that of feathers or other structures of the skin, or whether they look more like tissues that have started to decay after the animal died. We could examine fossils of

Top: The photograph shows the skin impression of a hadrosaur.
Bottom: The skeleton of *Caudipteryx*, a bird-like dinosaur or dinosaur-like bird from China, about 33 inches (85 cm) long. Arrows indicate feathers attached to the arm and tail.

ancient birds preserved in rocks, to see if fossilized feathers ever look like the fossilized fiber-like structures of *Sinosauropteryx*. We could also look at fossils of other animals from the same site as *Sinosauropteryx*. If fossils of animals without feathers or fur—such as frogs, lizards, or turtles—have structures like those seen in *Sinosauropteryx*, then the structures are probably not features of the animals' skin.

Interestingly, *Caudipteryx* and *Protarchaeopteryx*, two other ancient animals found in the same rocks as *Sinosauropteryx*, do have feathers preserved with their skeletons. Most paleontologists think that these animals were theropods. If so, perhaps *Sinosauropteryx*, and other theropods, did have feathers or feather-like structures at some time during their lives.

But wait—there is another possibility. A few paleontologists think that *Caudipteryx* and *Protarchaeopteryx* are not typical theropods, but are actually very primitive birds. If they are right, then we can't use *Caudipteryx* and *Protarchaeopteryx* to support the idea that *Sinosauropteryx* did have feather-like features. This is a matter about which there is vigorous argument. You might say the feathers are still flying here.

One thing we will probably never know about dinosaurs is exactly what color they were—although we may someday find extremely well-preserved dinosaur fossils that show us something about dark and light-colored areas of the skin. Living animals use color patterns in many ways: to hide in their surroundings, to help control their body temperatures, to advertise when they are ready to mate, and to warn **carnivores** (meat-eaters) that they are poisonous, taste bad, or are otherwise nasty. We suspect that the color patterns of dinosaurs served similar functions, but we have no way of knowing any dinosaur's color pattern. Some scientific artists give dinosaurs dull color patterns, like those of adult alligators and crocodiles. Other artists paint dinosaurs with bright colors, as seen in many lizards and birds. Actually, dinosaur color patterns are only educated guesses that reflect the artist's speculation.

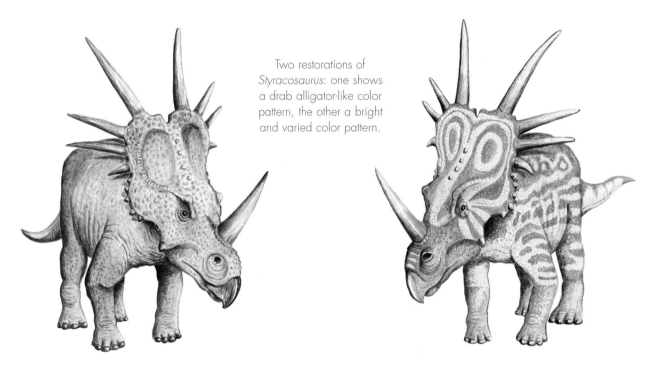

Two restorations of *Styracosaurus*: one shows a drab alligator-like color pattern, the other a bright and varied color pattern.

To sum up, paleontologists can be pretty sure about what a dinosaur's skeleton looked like if they have a fairly complete set of bones with which to work. We make educated guesses about what the dinosaur's internal organs and musculature were like, and sometimes well-preserved fossils guide us. Well-preserved dinosaur fossils also help us determine what the animals' skin was like, but sometimes scientists disagree over how the evidence should be interpreted. All our ideas about dinosaur color patterns are only speculation.

CHAPTER 3
WHAT DID DINOSAURS EAT?

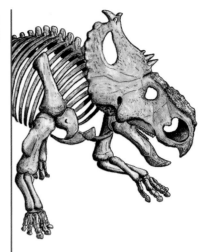

Naturally, finding food was an important part of every dinosaur's life. Paleontologists rely upon different kinds of clues to reconstruct dinosaur diets. First, we look at the teeth, jaws, and other parts of the body of modern **herbivores** (plant-eaters) or carnivores, to see how the shapes of body parts are related to animal diets. Once we understand the relation between body-part shape and diet, we can use this knowledge in interpreting dinosaur diets.

The teeth and jaws of modern carnivores and herbivores show many differences. Carnivore teeth often are knife-like, with sharp points and edges. They are used to hold, slash, or tear into the bodies of victims during an attack, and to cut meat from the prey animal's body once it is dead.

The joint connecting the upper and lower jaw is often in line with the teeth of the lower jaw. This makes a carnivore's jaws work like scissors. With scissors, the cutting force is concentrated on the spot where the two halves of the scissors meet, and then moves forward as the scissors close. Similarly, when a carnivore's jaws close, the teeth of

Side views of the skull and lower jaw of four animals: a cat (top left) and cow (top right), and *Allosaurus* (bottom left) and *Kritosaurus* (bottom right). Note the size and shape of the teeth, and the position of the jaw joint (arrows) relative to the tooth row.

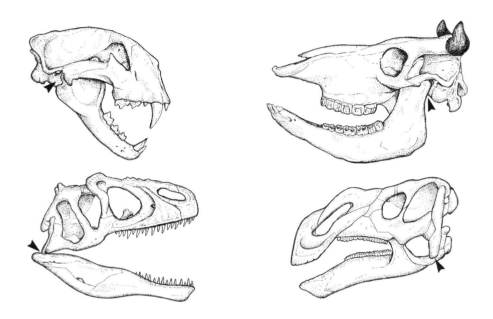

the upper and lower jaw come together, one after another, starting at the back of the jaws and moving forward. The bite force is concentrated at one spot along the jaws at a time. This increases the puncturing or cutting action of the teeth, and helps a carnivore to kill prey animals and tear meat from their bodies.

Although many living plant-eaters have sharp tusks that they use in fights with each other and with carnivores, their chewing teeth are not as sharp as carnivore teeth. Modern herbivorous lizards do not chew their food, but use their teeth to tear plants into bite-sized pieces that they then swallow whole. Most herbivorous mammals, however, have teeth that chop, grind, or slice their food into tiny pieces. The teeth of both the upper and lower jaw are not knife-shaped, but instead have large, flat surfaces that meet when the animal chews.

For herbivores that thoroughly chew their food, the jaw joint is not in line with the teeth. Thus, when the jaws come together, all the chewing teeth of the upper and lower jaws meet at nearly the same time. All the chewing surfaces work together, which makes the teeth more effective in breaking up plant materials.

Living carnivores and herbivores differ in more than their teeth and jaws. A carnivore's sharply curved claws can grab and hold prey while the meat-eater prepares to bite. In contrast, herbivores' toes usually bear blunt nails or hooves instead of sharp claws.

All the features that distinguish living herbivores from living carnivores can be seen in dinosaurs. Most theropods had sharp, knife-like teeth, usually with finely serrated edges like the cutting edges of modern shark teeth. The jaw joint in theropods was in line with the **tooth row** (the line of teeth from front to

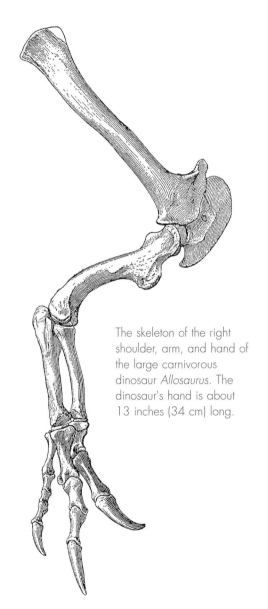

The skeleton of the right shoulder, arm, and hand of the large carnivorous dinosaur *Allosaurus*. The dinosaur's hand is about 13 inches (34 cm) long.

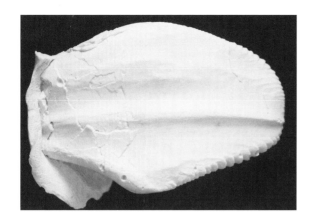

These two dinosaur tooth casts are from a plant-eating ornithopod (left), length about 1.8 inches (46 mm); and from a carnivorous tyrannosaur (below), length about 2.2 inches (56 mm). The tooth of the meat-eater is more pointed, with smaller serrations along its edge.

back in a jawbone). Theropod hands and feet had sharp claws; in some theropods, the **dromaeosaurids** and **troodontids**, the large inner toe of the hindfoot bore a huge claw that could slash the bodies of prey. These skeletal features strongly indicate that most theropods were carnivores.

Other dinosaurs, such as **prosauropods, sauropods, stegosaurs,** and **ankylosaurs,** had fairly simple, blunt-tipped, often spoon-shaped teeth. The edges of these teeth often have coarse serrations that are quite different from the finer serrations that give theropod teeth their sharp cutting edges. The jaw joint in prosauropods, sauropods, stegosaurs, and ankylosaurs is often below the level of the teeth. These observations suggest that these reptiles were plant-eaters.

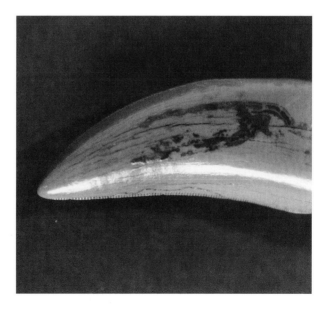

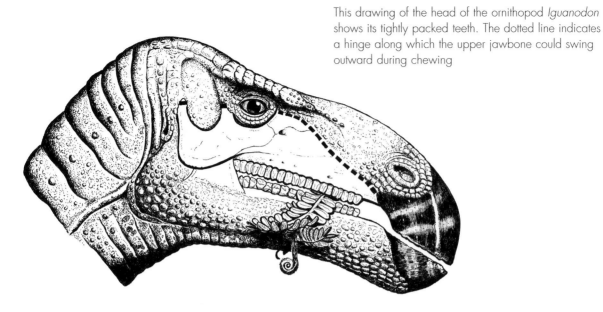

Food processing was more complicated in **ornithopods** and **ceratopsians**. Their teeth were tightly packed together in continuous rows, forming a grinding or slicing surface. The jaw joint was below the level of the tooth row. In most ornithopods the tooth-bearing bone of the upper jaw could swing outward as the jaws closed, giving these dinosaurs an unusual and effective chewing action. These features suggest that ornithopods and ceratopsians were herbivores that thoroughly chewed tough plant materials.

Many dinosaurs that we think were herbivores have their teeth located a bit inside the outer jaw surfaces. There are bony ridges above the outer surface of the upper tooth row and below the lower tooth row. What could this have accomplished? Paleontologists have speculated that cheek-like flaps of skin connected these ridges of the upper and lower jaws. As a dinosaur chewed, bits of plant material fell from the teeth and were trapped by the cheeks. The dinosaur could then use its tongue to sweep the collected food from its cheeks back into its mouth.

However, we do not see cheeks like this in any modern crocodilians or birds, the only living dinosaur relatives. This does not prove that herbivorous dinosaurs did not have cheeks, but we must look at the possibility that the bony ridges had some other function.

In modern birds and turtles, and also in the same **ornithischian** dinosaurs that have been thought to have cheeks, bones at the front ends of the upper and lower jaws have a rough surface appearance. In birds and turtles, this surface appearance indicates the presence of a beak made of horny material—like fingernails. Modern birds and turtles are toothless, and use their beaks to cut, crack, or tear their food. Ornithischians probably had similar beaks, used in the same way, to help process food. Perhaps the bony ridges around the ornithischians' tooth rows were related to the beaks also. They may have anchored especially large beaks that extended from the front of the mouth back around the jaws.

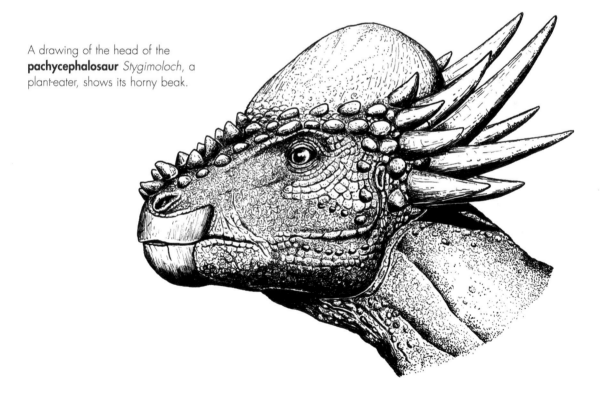

A drawing of the head of the **pachycephalosaur** *Stygimoloch*, a plant-eater, shows its horny beak.

With no teeth, herbivorous birds cannot chew their food. However, there is a very muscular region in birds' digestive systems that rubs against and grinds food items. Birds swallow sand and bits of stone that collect in this region of the gut, and these hard materials help to break down food. The sand grains and stones act like teeth inside the bird's body.

Skeletons of some **ornithomimids**, prosauropods, sauropods, and ceratopsians have been found with collections of stones in the region where the gut would have been. It seems likely that the stones helped in food processing for these dinosaurs, as they do for birds.

Plant materials are often made of tough fibers that are hard to digest, and many plant leaves contain chemicals that are poisonous to animals. Modern herbivorous animals have large digestive systems with special chambers where bacteria and protozoa live. These microscopic creatures chemically attack the plant fibers and change poisonous materials into harmless substances. Herbivorous animals would have trouble digesting food without them. To provide room for the enlarged

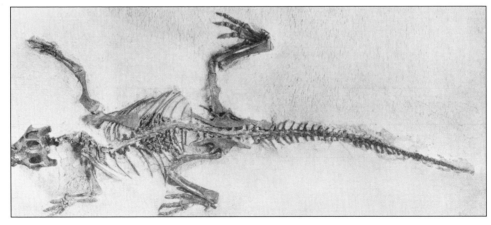

This skeleton of the small, herbivorous dinosaur *Psittacosaurus* was found with gastroliths (stones) in the stomach region. The living animal was about 55 inches (140 cm) long.

digestive chambers, modern herbivores have broad, often barrel-shaped bodies.

If the dinosaurs that we think were herbivores did eat plants, they too would have needed big guts to digest them. In fact, their bodies were broad, and sometimes long, in the gut region. This is more evidence for thinking that these dinosaurs were herbivores.

If we look at the feet of the dinosaurs that we think ate plants, we find that their toes usually have blunt, hoof-like tips instead of sharp claws. Even with those that do have clawed toes, the foot is not constructed in a way that would allow the claw to be useful in capturing prey. Unlike the clawed fingers and toes of theropods, the toes of these dinosaurs look more like those of modern plant-eaters.

These interpretations about dinosaur diets are based on comparisons between dinosaurs and living animals. When we look at a dinosaur skeleton and see many features shared by modern carnivorous animals, for example, we confidently conclude that our dinosaur was a meat-eater. It is especially helpful when different parts of the dinosaur's skeleton all suggest the same thing about what the dinosaur ate. When this happens, we can think of our interpretation as a well-supported hypothesis. Even so, it is nice if we can find other kinds of evidence to test these hypotheses about dinosaur diets.

Nature sometimes gives us such other kinds of evidence. Dinosaur bones have been found that are scarred by bite marks that match the size and shape of theropod teeth. One bone even had an embedded piece of a theropod's tooth. It probably broke off after the dinosaur bit into the prey animal's bone. A few theropod skeletons have been found that contain bones from their last dinners. We can therefore be certain that we are correct in identifying these dinosaurs as meat-eaters!

Two views of a piece of hadrosaur leg bone. Left: Tooth marks scratch the surface of the bone. Note the red arrow at the end of the bone. When the bone is turned (right), the arrow indicates the tooth of a carnivorous dinosaur embedded in the bone. The exposed portion of the tooth is about 1/4-inch (5 mm) long.

Under the right conditions, dinosaur droppings can be converted to stone. These fossils, **coprolites**, tell us a lot about dinosaur diets. Some coprolites contain pieces of fibrous plant leaves and stems. We cannot be certain which dinosaur left the coprolite (we obviously can't watch it happening), but these coprolites have been found in rock formations along with the skeletons of dinosaurs whose teeth suggest that they ate just such fibrous plant materials.

If we are lucky, the evidence from bite marks, stomach contents, and coprolites agrees with interpretations of what dinosaurs ate based on skeletal evidence. If so, we can be confident that we have identified a dinosaur as a meat-eater or plant-eater, and we regard this interpretation as a theory, or even as a fact that might be useful in testing other hypotheses.

Some dinosaurs' diets are still a mystery. Certain theropods (ornithomimids and **oviraptorosaurs**) had toothless jaws. Did they eat plants, or small animals, or anything that they could swallow? Perhaps we will someday find skeletons of these dinosaurs with food items in the gut region, and be able to answer these questions.

CHAPTER 4
HOW DID DINOSAURS FIGHT?

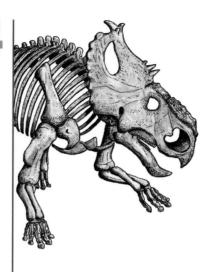

In nature, animals fight for a variety of reasons: to kill prey, to defend themselves against predators, to win mates, and to protect their own **territories**. Animals are equipped with many fighting weapons. Carnivores have teeth and claws; herbivores have hooves, tusks, and horns they can use with deadly results.

Some fights are between members of the same species. Usually these are disputes between male animals over females, or over territories where the males' families will be reared. Often, though, fights between rival males are avoided by **displays** that advertise the size and fighting condition of aggressive animals. Once an animal sees how tough its rival is, it may then not waste time and energy on a fight it can't win. Males also use displays to attract females. We see that the body structures animals use in displays—such as horns or antlers—are usually bigger and more impressive in males than in females of the same species.

Male deer turn their heads from side to side, showing the size and complex shapes of their antlers. Male birds warn off rivals by their

singing and their bright feathers. Frogs sing during the mating season, and inflate their throat sacs. Alligators bellow with such intensity that the water around them shakes.

The display structures of different animal species vary by size, shape, and color. Displays that involve songs and calls are different for each species. Because of these differences, females can use displays to identify males of their own species for mating.

We know how display structures are used by living animals, and so, when we see similar features in dinosaurs, we suspect that dinosaurs used these structures in the same way. Since we can't observe dinosaur displays, these interpretations are only hypotheses. However, we can test our hypotheses by seeing if those observations that we can make support them.

Many **hadrosaurs** had big, bony crests atop their heads. Different hadrosaur species had crests of different shapes. These differences lead us to speculate that hadrosaurs used crest shapes to identify members of their own kind during the mating season. Within one hadrosaur species, some individuals have larger, showier crests than others. Because of what we observe in living animals, we think that the bigger-crested hadrosaurs were males.

This is a hypothesis about hadrosaur crests. It is hard to test this hypothesis, but we can try to imagine a way to test it. For example, we know that hadrosaurs laid eggs (see chapter 5). If someday we find a hadrosaur skeleton with fossilized eggs inside its body, we could identify our hadrosaur as a female who died before egg-laying. If that female had

Presumed female (left) and male (right) of the hadrosaur *Lambeosaurus*

a small crest, this observation would support our hypothesis that male hadrosaurs used their crests to attract females. But, if our female hadrosaur had a big, showy crest, this would show that our speculation that males had bigger crests than females was wrong. We might have to throw out the hypothesis that hadrosaur crests were display structures, or maybe change it to suggest that it was the females who displayed their crests to attract males!

Paleontologists speculate about another possible use of hadrosaur crests. Hadrosaur crests were hollow, with air passages running from the hadrosaur's nose into the crest, and then down into the dinosaur's throat. Hadrosaurs could therefore have blown air through their crests. The size and shape of these air tubes is like that of some musical instruments. Perhaps hadrosaurs used their crests to make honking or trumpeting sounds. Because the crests were of different shapes in different hadrosaur species, each species could have made its own sound.

This hypothesis, too, is hard to test. However, it is interesting to note that the size and shape of hadrosaur ear bones indicate that these dinosaurs probably had good hearing. This observation isn't a true test of our singing hadrosaur hypothesis, but it supports the hypothesis. If hadrosaur ears were unable to hear much, why would these reptiles have been able to make interesting noises through their crests?

Like hadrosaurs, ceratopsians may have used their heads for visual displays. Bony frills project from the back of the ceratopsian skull, and different species of ceratopsians have skulls decorated with combinations of long or short eye and nose horns, and spikes or knobs along the margins of their frills. The ceratopsians we think were males have larger, showier frills than those we think were females of the same species. Also, studies of young and adult specimens of the same ceratopsian

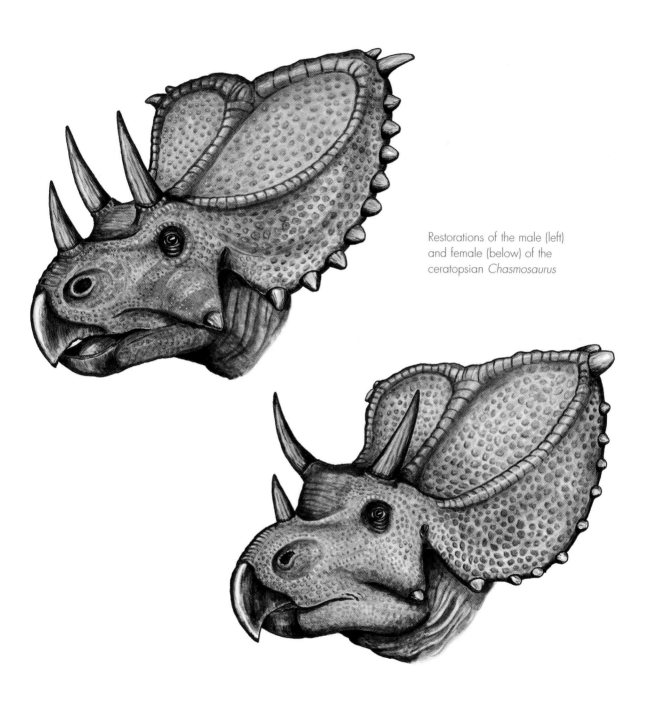

Restorations of the male (left)
and female (below) of the
ceratopsian *Chasmosaurus*

species show that horns and frills were unimpressive until the dinosaurs had grown to mating size. This supports the hypothesis that horns and frills were important in their mating behavior.

Like modern deer and antelope, ceratopsians may have waved their horns and frills about to attract females and warn off rival males. If a rival did not leave the area, however, ceratopsians could back up their displays with physical force. Modern animals with horns or antlers—deer, antelope, and chameleon lizards—fight with their prickly headgear. An animal may try to stab an opponent with its horns, and the opponent may catch the attacker's horns with its own. The two animals then shove and twist until one of them tires and moves away. Because ceratopsian horns are so similar to those of antelope and chameleons, it seems likely that ceratopsians used their horns to fight also.

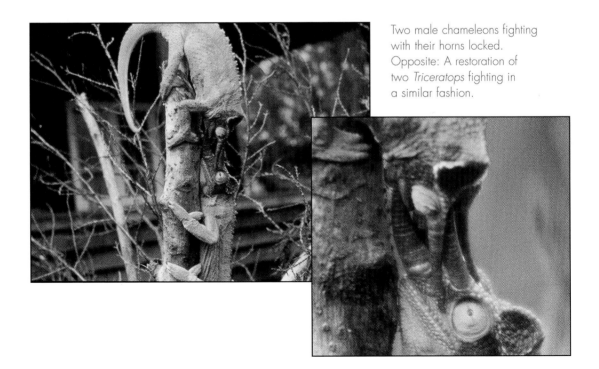

Two male chameleons fighting with their horns locked. Opposite: A restoration of two *Triceratops* fighting in a similar fashion.

Some ceratopsian skulls have holes that look like puncture wounds, although some paleontologists think the holes were caused by other injuries or disease. For some ceratopsian species, we have found bones of many different individuals, and among these bones there is little evidence of horn-related injuries. This is a puzzle: If the horns were used for fighting, shouldn't horn-related injuries be pretty common? Perhaps ceratopsians just weren't as aggressive as their ferocious appearance leads us to think.

Many of our interpretations about how dinosaurs displayed and fought are based on comparisons with modern animals. These ideas are hard to test. Sometimes other features of the dinosaur's skeleton support our interpretation—as in the case of the ear bones of hadrosaurs. But other times, as with the ceratopsian puncture wounds, we haven't found separate evidence to either support our ideas or to prove them wrong. There is a lot more to learn about how dinosaurs fought.

CHAPTER 5
HOW DID DINOSAURS REPRODUCE AND GROW?

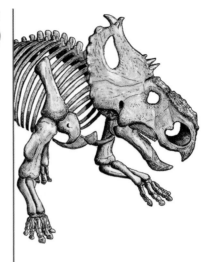

The closest living relatives of dinosaurs are birds and crocodilians. These dinosaur relatives all reproduce by laying eggs. It is therefore likely that most—and probably all—dinosaurs were egg-layers as well.

Some living animals lay eggs with soft or flexible shells, while others lay hard-shelled eggs. All known dinosaur eggs are hard-shelled, but we don't know whether this is because all dinosaur species laid hard-shelled eggs, or whether hard-shelled eggs are more likely to fossilize.

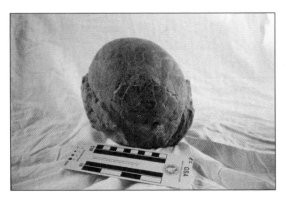 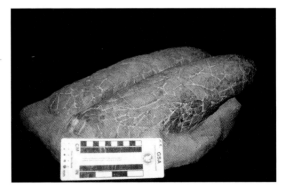

Dinosaur eggs vary by species. Left: a possible hadrosaur egg. Right: possible large theropod eggs.

We have found eggs that were probably laid by many different dinosaur species, but unfortunately, we can rarely say for sure which kind of dinosaur laid which egg. To identify the egg-layer, we'd need to find identifiable bones of baby dinosaurs in unhatched eggs, or in nests alongside pieces of eggshell; or the skeleton of a parent dinosaur preserved with its nest.

The story of *Oviraptor* is a good lesson in why we need to be cautious in identifying an egg-layer. The first skeleton of *Oviraptor* found was with a nest of fossilized eggs. Because the small ceratopsian *Protoceratops* is the most common dinosaur in the rocks where the nest was found, scientists thought that the eggs must have belonged to *Protoceratops*. They concluded that the *Oviraptor* had been trying to eat the eggs and was killed by an angry *Protoceratops.* (The name *Oviraptor* means "egg thief.") More recently, however, adult oviraptorosaur skeletons have been found preserved sitting on nests of the same kind of egg, and tiny oviraptorosaur skeletons have been found inside the eggs. Instead of stealing another dinosaur's eggs, the oviraptorosaurs seem to have been killed, perhaps by sandstorms or by collapsing sand dunes, while guarding or incubating their own eggs!

Once their eggs hatch, parents of most species of birds and crocodilians provide some protection and care for their young. Baby crocodilians stay together with a parent nearby. If a predator threatens, a baby crocodilian grunts a call that brings adults rushing to its defense. Some baby birds are ready to leave the nest soon after hatching, but remain near their parents for safety. In other bird species the young are helpless for a long time after hatching, and parents bring them food. Is there evidence of this kind of behavior in dinosaurs?

Skeletons of babies of the hadrosaur *Maiasaura* have been found preserved in nests. Some paleontologists think that these little dinosaurs' limbs were not well-enough developed to allow them to move very far

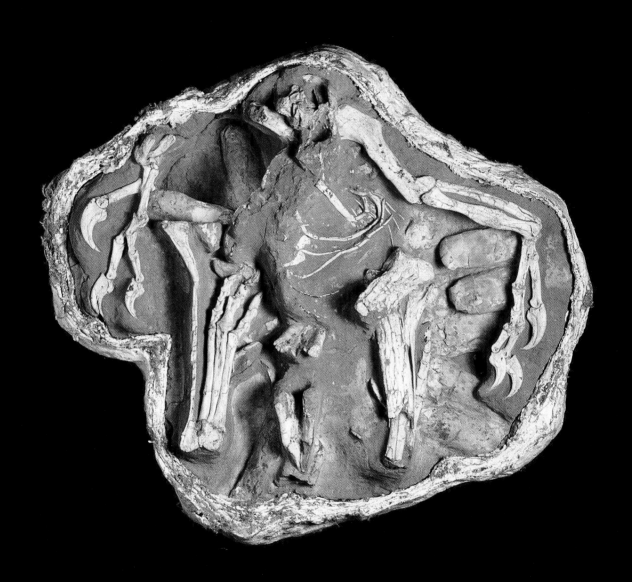

This small theropod dinosaur, *Oviraptor*, was preserved sitting on its nest. Each egg (seen at the right) is about 7 inches (18 cm) long.

on their own. They believe that baby *Maiasaura* stayed in the nest, with their parents bringing them food. Other scientists, however, argue that the legs of baby *Maiasaura* were as well developed as those of baby birds that can walk around right after hatching. If baby *Maiasaura* did leave the nest, perhaps they returned at night to sleep, or when threatened.

Bonebeds are fossil finds in which large numbers of dinosaur bones, often of the same species, occur in one place. Bonebeds often record the sudden deaths of many individual dinosaurs in a disaster, such as a drought or flood. Often the dinosaurs are of different sizes, and probably different ages, suggesting that young and adult animals of the same species lived in the same group. Bonebeds of this kind are known for hadrosaurs such as *Maiasaura*, ceratopsians such as *Centrosaurus*, and theropods such as *Coelophysis* and *Allosaurus*.

Bones exposed in a hadrosaur bonebed, Dinosaur Provincial Park, Alberta, Canada

Fossil footprints provide more evidence that young and old dinosaurs of some species lived together. Fossilized trackways of large and small sauropods have been found together at the same site, all heading in the same direction. The footprints differ only in size. This suggests that the trackways were made by different-aged individuals of the same sauropod species. They may have been traveling in a single herd. If young and adult individuals of the same species lived together, the adults may have provided some defense of the young, as living crocodilians and birds do.

Information about how animals grow is preserved in their bones. In slowly growing bone, the texture is dense, with few blood vessels in the bone tissue. Bone tissues of this kind are common in living reptiles. In many modern reptiles, growth slows or stops during a cold or otherwise difficult season. These times of slowed growth are shown by circular lines in the bone, called **lines of arrested growth**. These lines look a bit like the rings we see in tree trunks.

Rapidly growing bone, which is common in modern birds and mammals, has a more open texture, with more spaces for blood vessels. In birds and mammals, growth rarely slows down enough to produce lines of arrested growth.

Dinosaur bone usually has the open texture that is characteristic of rapidly growing bone. In some dinosaurs, though, bones show obvious lines of arrested growth. This suggests that these dinosaurs grew at fairly rapid rates, but that there were times when growth slowed or stopped.

It is one thing to say that dinosaur growth rates were fast, but harder to say just *how* fast. Can we determine how much dinosaurs increased their body length or weight per day, or how long it took them to reach maturity?

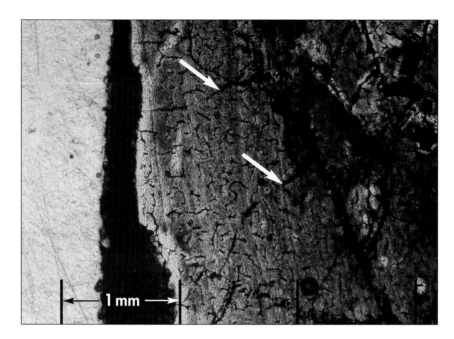

Photographs show thin sections of limb bones of *Syntarsus* (left), and *Dryosaurus (below)*. Lines of arrested growth (arrows) can be seen in the bone of *Syntarsus*, but not that of *Dryosaurus*. The scale bars equal 1 millimeter in each photo.

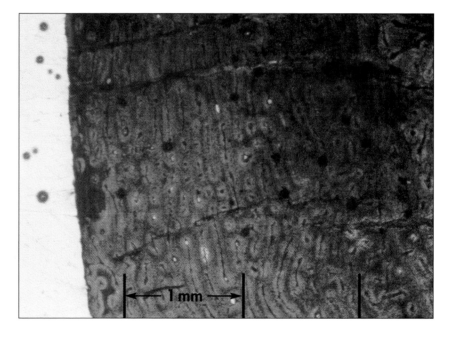

A spectacular bonebed in Montana contains the remains of hundreds or even thousands of individuals of the hadrosaur *Maiasaura*. Certain sizes of dinosaur are more common than others in the bonebed. This pattern could occur if all the *Maiasaura* laid their eggs at the same time every year. Each of the common *Maiasaura* sizes could represent animals that hatched in one particular year. By counting the number of common sizes in the bonebed, we get an idea of how many years it took for *Maiasaura* to grow to full size. Using this count, we estimate that *Maiasaura* grew to the size of an elephant in only four or five years—a very fast growth rate! However, this interpretation assumes that all of the year classes in the life cycle of *Maiasaura* were represented in the bonebed, and we can't be sure of that.

If lines of arrested growth in dinosaur bone formed only once a year, then a count of these lines can give us an estimate of how long it took a dinosaur to grow to the size it was at the time it died. Paleontologists have estimated that the small theropod *Syntarsus* took 7 to 8 years, the prosauropod *Massospondylus* 15 years, and *Maiasaura* 6 to 7 years to reach full size. Using the same method, the small theropod *Troodon* was thought to have reached full size in 3 to 5 years.

Once again, however, these estimates of dinosaur growth rates depend on some assumptions—this time that the lines of arrested growth formed only once a year, and that all of the yearly lines of arrested growth are recorded in the dinosaur bones. If these assumptions are incorrect, the true growth rates of the dinosaurs could have been much faster or slower. Furthermore, some dinosaurs, such as **dryosaurs**, have bone textures that suggest rapid growth, but show no lines of arrested growth. Growth rates in these dinosaurs may have been rapid and continuous, although for now we have no way of knowing just how fast they were.

Our present understanding of how dinosaurs reproduced and grew mixes observations, speculations, and hypotheses. We know which dinosaurs laid certain eggs, but for most eggs, all we can now do is make educated guesses about who laid them. Nests, bonebeds, and tracksites make us think that some dinosaur species provided some protection and care for their young, but we don't know how much. We can estimate the growth rates of some dinosaurs, but we work from assumptions that may or may not be true. It is best to think of these growth rates as hypotheses. It would be nice to have other ways of estimating growth rates so we could test these hypotheses. We have a lot to learn about dinosaur reproduction and growth.

CHAPTER 6
LOOKING AT A HYPOTHESIS:
HOW DID
STEGOSAURUS
USE ITS PLATES?

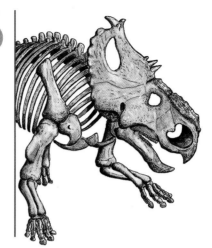

To sum up the way paleontologists think about dinosaur biology, let's look at a specific, and rather complicated, case: What was the function of the peculiar bony plates that covered the back of the herbivorous dinosaur *Stegosaurus*?

From the time *Stegosaurus* was first found, its flat, bony plates have been interpreted as defensive armor that protected the dinosaur from the attacks of carnivorous dinosaurs. Spines on the tail of *Stegosaurus*, and on the back and tail of other stegosaurs, are sharp, strong bones that certainly look like useful weapons. So weren't the plates part of the same system of defense?

It may be that the plates protected the dinosaur's back, particularly if the bone of the plates was covered by a surface layer of horn. However, some features of the plates are puzzling if these structures were only body armor. Why are they so tall and thin? Why are they made of bone with an open, spongy texture, filled with spaces for blood vessels, and heavily grooved by blood vessels on their outer surfaces? Wouldn't short, thick plates of dense bone make better armor? And why

A reconstruction of *Stegosaurus stenops*

A photograph of a large, bony plate from the back of *Stegosaurus*. The plate is about 26 inches (66 cm) long. Note the vertical grooves for blood vessels along the top of the plate. The inset shows a cross-section of *Stegosaurus* plate from the area near its tip. The dark curved areas are actual bone; the lighter areas are spaces that would have been filled by soft materials, including blood vessels.

are the plates arranged in an alternating pattern along the dinosaur's back, instead of being paired, like the spikes on the dinosaur's tail?

Another hypothesis is that the plates were display structures, to make stegosaurs look bigger and more threatening to other stegosaurs—

and maybe predators, too. Many living lizards have frills along their backs, and some hadrosaurs and sauropods had similar frills or rows of spines along their backs that could have been used this way. Furthermore, different stegosaur species had different arrangements of plates and spines along their backs, which is what we would expect if each species had its own pattern of back ornaments for display purposes.

The display explanation is appealing, but how can we test it? If males and females of the same *Stegosaurus* species had different plate sizes and arrangements, this would be strong supporting evidence. So far we have no information about this. If the plates had been movable, so that the dinosaur could raise and lower or wiggle them, this would be consistent with the way that many modern animals use display structures. However, the bone texture of the plate surface indicates that the plates probably were not movable, but were firmly embedded in the dinosaur's skin.

The presence of blood vessels on the bony surface of the plates, which in life would have been covered by skin or horn, suggests that the dinosaur might have been able to flush the plates with blood, and perhaps suddenly change their color. We see this in displays of living animals. However it is a hard hypothesis to test since we have no information about dinosaur color patterns and how changeable they were. For now, the display hypothesis is attractive, but the supporting evidence is weak.

Another possibility is that the plates were used as cooling fins. When the dinosaur's body became too warm, blood could be pumped into the plates. As breezes blew around the plates, they cooled them, just as a radiator cools a car's engine. The cooled blood then flowed back into the dinosaur's body, lowering its temperature.

Various plate and spine arrangements on stegosaurs, including (from the top): *Stegosaurus armatus*, *Kentrosaurus*, *Tuojiangosaurus*, and *Huayangosaurus*.

This "cooling fin" hypothesis is consistent with the shape of the larger plates on the back of *Stegosaurus*. A flat, thin object cools more quickly than a thick, rounded object does. It is also consistent with the thin, spongy texture of the plates, a texture that probably indicates the presence of many blood vessels on the surface and inside the plates.

Most interesting of all, experiments with model stegosaurs show that the alternating arrangement of plates is ideal for dumping body heat to cooling breezes. More heat can be dumped if the plates are alternating than if they are paired. With alternating plates, the dinosaur can benefit from breezes coming from any direction. It doesn't have to shift its position to catch the breeze, as it would if the fins were paired. Furthermore, the largest plates of *Stegosaurus* were near the top of its back, where breezes would be stronger than they would be closer to the ground.

The cooling fin hypothesis has a lot going for it, but it also has weaknesses. If large dinosaurs such as *Stegosaurus* were so likely to overheat that cooling fins were useful, why don't we see them in many different kinds of dinosaurs? And, why did some species of *Stegosaurus* have fairly small plates in comparison with their body size, unlike the species upon which the cooling experiments were based? And why did stegosaurs other than *Stegosaurus* have entirely different plate and spine arrangements?

Of course, the same objections can be raised with other hypotheses about the purpose of the plates. For example, if the plates were used for defense, why could some species of *Stegosaurus* protect themselves with fairly small plates when other species could not? Why did *Stegosaurus* need plates for protection when other groups of dinosaurs didn't?

The cooling fin explanation for the plates of *Stegosaurus* does as good a job of explaining some features of the plates, such as their thin shape, as any other hypothesis. It does a better job of explaining the alternating arrangement of the plates than any other hypothesis. However, it does not explain other facts quite as well.

This could mean that the cooling fin hypothesis is incorrect. Or, the hypothesis may be only part of the explanation of *Stegosaurus* plates. Perhaps the plates had more than one function—such as both cooling and display. Maybe the cooling fin function was most important for the big-plated species of *Stegosaurus*.

The external ears of the two living species of elephants give us a useful comparison. Both the African and the Asian elephant wave their ears back and forth to communicate with other members of their species. Although the African elephant's ears are much bigger than those of the Asian elephant, both species also flap their thin ears to dump body heat. Perhaps, like elephant ears, *Stegosaurus* plates had more than one function.

CHAPTER 7
WORKING TO UNDERSTAND WHAT DINOSAURS WERE LIKE

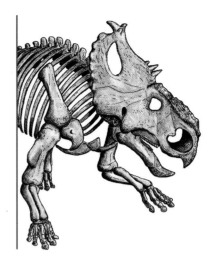

The *Stegosaurus* plate story shows how hard it is to develop well-supported theories about dinosaur biology. No explanation of the plates is clearly supported by all our observations and experiments. And, if the plates played more than one role in the life of the dinosaur, it may be difficult to determine which function had the greatest effect on the shape, size, and arrangement of the plates.

Trying to understand what dinosaurs were like involves a lot of work in the field and the laboratory—and more than a little hard thinking about whether observations support or prove wrong any particular idea about dinosaurs! Let us summarize what we have learned about thinking about dinosaurs.

- First, interpretations about dinosaurs that are based on direct observations of bones—such as ideas about body size or diet—are the ones about which we can be most confident, particularly if different kinds of evidence lead us to the same conclusion.

- Hypotheses about dinosaur behavior or body temperature control, that are less directly based on fossils and that require comparisons

49

with modern animals or laboratory experiments on model dinosaurs, can sometimes be tested. However, we can't be as confident as we are when the interpretations are based directly on the fossils.

- Some speculations about dinosaur biology, such as estimates of growth rates, may be reasonable, but very hard—or even impossible—to test.

- Our ideas about what dinosaurs were like as living animals will probably always be a mixture of observations, theories, hypotheses, and educated guesses.

Fortunately, new dinosaur fossils are being discovered every day, and each new find may provide crucial evidence for testing a hypothesis. New techniques of studying fossils now allow us to test hypotheses in ways that were once impossible.

For example, computers are increasingly important in paleontologists' efforts to understand how dinosaur skeletons worked as living machines. Computer models of the tail bones of sauropods such as *Apatosaurus* suggest that these dinosaurs could have cracked their tails like whips, making loud noises that might have been used in displays. Scientists also use computers to estimate the amount of movement possible between the bone joints in sauropod necks. These studies may tell us how high different species of sauropods could raise their necks while feeding.

However, you don't have to be a paleontologist, or have the world's most powerful computer, to think critically about dinosaurs. When you hear a paleontologist make statements about what a particular

A computer-generated model of the sauropod *Diplodocus* shows the maximum degree to which it could raise its head, as determined by computer analysis of the joints between the neck bones.

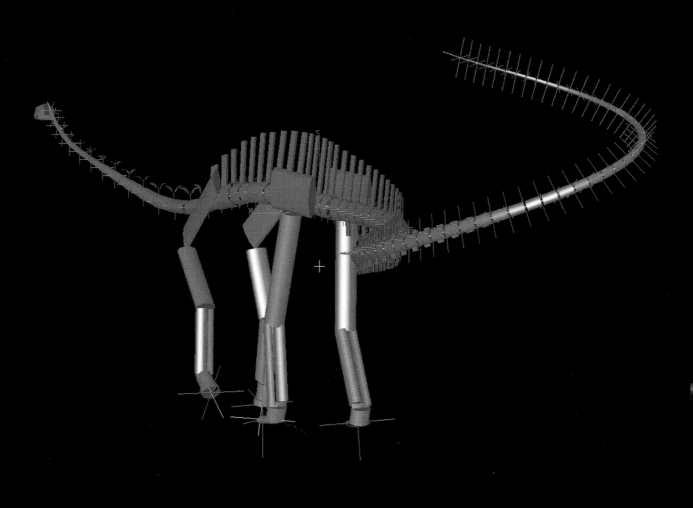

A scientific artist's view of life in the time of the dinosaurs

dinosaur was like, ask yourself these questions: What observations led the scientist to make those interpretations? How has the scientist tested the ideas? Are there other observations or experiments that could further test those ideas? Are the paleontologist's ideas best regarded as observations, hypotheses, or simple guesses? If you ask questions of this kind, and don't accept what the scientist says just because he or she is a scientist, then you will be thinking about dinosaurs in a scientific way yourself.

GLOSSARY

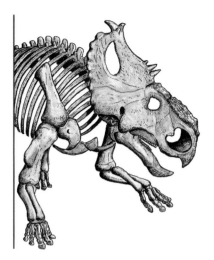

Ankylosaurs (ang-kye'-lo-sores)—ornithischian dinosaurs armored by thick bony bumps and plates on the tops of their heads, backs, and tails.

Bonebeds—fossil finds in which large numbers of bones are found together in one place.

Carnivores (car'-nih-vors)—animals that eat meat.

Ceratopsians (sair-uh-top'-see-uns)—horned dinosaurs and their relatives; one of the groups of ornithischians.

Coprolites (cop'-roh-lites)—fossilized animal droppings.

Displays—postures, movements, songs, and other behaviors by which animals advertise their size, strength, and willingness to mate or to fight.

Dromaeosaurids (droh'-mee-oh-sor-ids)—small to medium-sized theropods, such as *Dromaeosaurus, Deinonychus,* and *Velociraptor,* that had big claws on the inner toes of their feet.

Dryosaurs (dry'-oh-sors)—a group of small to medium-sized ornithopods.

Fossils—remains of ancient plants or animals, or traces of their presence and activities.

Hadrosaurs (had'-roh-sors)—a group of large ornithopods, often called "duckbilled" dinosaurs.

Herbivore (er'-bih-vor)—an animal that eats plants.

Hypothesis (hye-poth'-iss-us)—an educated guess about how something in nature works that can be tested by experiments or observations.

Interpretation—an explanation about a specimen that is based on study of the specimen, but cannot be directly observed (compare with observation).

Lines of arrested growth—marks inside dinosaur bone that indicate times when growth of the bone slowed or stopped.

Musculature (muss'-kyul-uh-choor)—the way that muscles are arranged on an animal's body.

Observation—a fact about a specimen that can be directly observed on that specimen.

Ornithischians (or-nith-iss'-kee-ans)—one of the main groups of dinosaurs. Ornithischians include stegosaurs, ankylosaurs, ornithopods, pachycephalosaurs, and ceratopsians.

Ornithomimosaurs (or-nith-oh-mim'-oh-sors)—long-necked, long-legged, usually toothless, small to medium-sized theropods.

Ornithopods (or-nith'-oh-pods)—a group of ornithischians (including dryosaurs, hadrosaurs, and their relatives) that could walk on two or four legs, and had a complicated tooth system capable of grinding plant food.

Oviraptorosaurs (oh-vih-rap'-tor-oh-sors)—small theropods such as *Oviraptor* that had strong, toothless beaks.

Pachycephalosaurs (pack-ee-seff'-uh-loh-sors)—ornithischians closely related to ceratopsians, characterized by thick domes of bone on top of their skulls.

Paleontologists (pay-lee-un-toll'-oh-jists)—scientists who study fossils to learn about prehistoric creatures and how they evolved.

Prosauropods (pro-sor'-oh-pods)—medium-sized to large, long-necked, plant-eating dinosaurs closely related to sauropods.

Reconstruction—an interpretation of what the skeleton of an extinct animal looked like.

Restoration—an interpretation of what an extinct creature looked like as a living animal.

Sauropods (sor'-oh-pods)—huge, long-necked, plant-eating dinosaurs closely related to prosauropods, and more distantly to theropods.

Stegosaurs (steg'-oh-sors)—a group of ornithischians characterized by rows of bony plates and or spines along their backs and tails.

Tendons—tissues that attach muscles to bones.

Territories—pieces of habitat that animals will try to keep other animals of their own species, and sometimes other species, from using.

Theory—an explanation about how something in nature works that has been tested many times by experiments and hypotheses, and never been disproved. A theory is therefore likely to be a true explanation. The scientific definition of a theory is different from the way many people use the word in everyday language, where it means a guess, with little hard evidence to support it.

Theropods (thair'-oh-pods)—meat-eating dinosaurs and their close relatives.

Tooth row—the line of teeth in an animal's jaw.

Troodontids (troh-oh-don'-tids)— a group of small theropods with large brains and big eyes.

FOR MORE INFORMATION

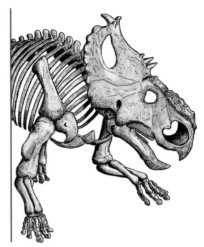

Books

Bennett, S. Christopher. *Pterosaurs: The Flying Reptiles.* New York: Franklin Watts, 1995.

Dewan, Ted. *Inside Dinosaurs and Other Prehistoric Creatures.* London: Dorling Kindersley, 1993.

Dixon, Dougal. *Dougal Dixon's Dinosaurs.* Honesdale, PA: Boyds Mills Press, 1993.

Eyewitness Visual Dictionaries. *The Visual Dictionary of Dinosaurs.* London: Dorling Kindersley, 1993.

Farlow, James O. *On the Tracks of Dinosaurs: A Study of Dinosaur Footprints.* New York: Franklin Watts, 1991.

Farlow, James O., and Ralph E. Molnar. *The Great Hunters: Meat-Eating Dinosaurs and Their World*. New York: Franklin Watts, 1995.

Gillette, J. Lynette. *The Search for Seismosaurus, The World's Longest Dinosaur*. New York: Dial Books for Young Readers, 1994.

Henderson, Douglas. *Dinosaur Tree.* New York: Bradbury Press, 1994.

Lessem, Don. *Dinosaur Worlds: New Dinosaurs, New Discoveries.* Honesdale, PA: Boyds Mills Press, 1996.

Weishampel, David B. *Plant-Eating Dinosaurs.* New York: Franklin Watts, 1992.

Witmer, Lawrence, M. *The Search for the Origin of Birds.* New York: Franklin Watts, 1995.

Internet Resources

The American Museum of Natural History
http://www.amnh.org/exhibitions/fossil_halls/index.html

The Field Museum of Natural History
http://www.fmnh.org/

The Hunterian Museum, University of Glasgow
http://www.gla.ac.uk/Museum/HuntMus/dinosaur/index.html

The Museum of Paleontology, University of California, Berkeley
http://www.ucmp.berkeley.edu/

The New Mexico Museum of Natural History and Science
http://www.nmmnh-abq.mus.nm.us/nmmnh/nmmnh.html

The Royal Tyrrell Museum of Palaeontology
http://www.tyrrellmuseum.com

INDEX

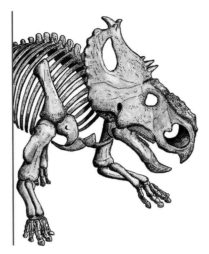

About the Author

James O. Farlow is a gifted interpreter of dinosaur science for young readers. He studied at Indiana University and at Yale University, where he earned a Ph.D. in geology, and is now on the faculty of the Department of Geosciences at Indiana–Purdue University in Fort Wayne, Indiana. He has published many scientific articles and appears often in television documentaries dealing with the great reptiles.

Dr. Farlow is the author of *The Great Hunters: Meat-Eating Dinosaurs and Their World* (with Ralph E. Molnar, Ph.D.), and *On the Tracks of Dinosaurs: A Study of Dinosaur Footprints*, both published by Franklin Watts; and is co-editor of *The Complete Dinosaur* (Indiana University Press).

James Farlow at work, measuring the thighbone of *Deinosuchus*, a huge crocodile that lived in the time of the dinosaurs.